published by planetOh concepts verlag
www.planetohconcepts.com

Publisher`s Note:
Please note that the Spanish and English versions of the story were written to be as close as possible. However, in some cases they may differ in order to accomodate the nuances and fluidity of each language. Author, translator, and publisher made every effort to ensure accuracy. We therefore take no responsibility for inconsistency and minor errors.

Illustrated by Mark Nino Balita
Book layout by Emy Farella
Translated by Fátima de los Ángeles Báez Santana
Proofread by Carmen Vargas Breval

First Edition 2021
ISBN: 979-8-695318-40-1

Ingo Blum

DON'T BE SCARED!

¡No tengas miedo!

Illustrated by
Mark Nino Balita

BILINGUAL
ENGLISH | SPANISH

Today, Susie's mother wants to bake a cake for the family.

She sends Susie to the village to get some butter, flour, and cherries for the cake.

But Susie is scared.

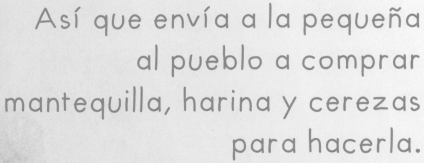

La mamá de Susie quiere preparar hoy una tarta para la familia.

Así que envía a la pequeña al pueblo a comprar mantequilla, harina y cerezas para hacerla.

Pero Susie tiene miedo.

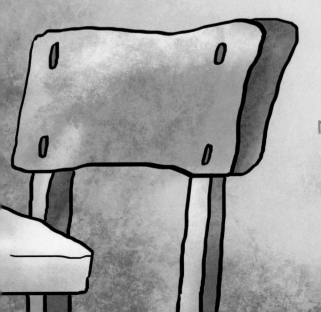

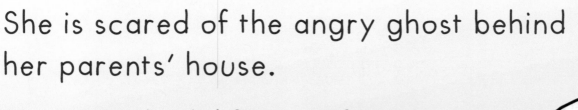

She is scared of the angry ghost behind her parents' house.

Tiene miedo del furioso fantasma que se esconde detrás de la casa de sus padres.

When she crosses a big field of barley, she hears a whisper. The whisper comes from the scarecrows in the field, who seem to be watching Susie.

Cuando cruza un extenso campo de cebada, oye un susurro. El susurro proviene de los espantapájaros del campo, que parecen estar observándola.

She is scared of the forest because it is dark and full of mysterious shadows.

Tiene miedo del bosque porque está oscuro y lleno de misteriosas sombras.

Look! There is a monster watching her with big yellow eyes. It has a huge mouth with sharp teeth.

But hold on, that's not a monster at all!

¡Mira! Hay un monstruo que la está mirando con unos grandes ojos amarillos. Y tiene una boca enorme con afilados dientes.

Pero espera, ¡no se trata de ningún monstruo!

It is a woman from the village.

"Where are you going, little Susie?" the woman asks with a smile.

"I am going to the village to get some ingredients for a cake."

Es una señora del pueblo.

—¿Adónde vas, pequeña Susie? —pregunta la señora mientras sonríe.

—Voy al pueblo a buscar unos ingredientes para hacer una tarta.

Susie is so scared of wolves.
Especially that wolf behind the fence!

A Susie le dan mucho miedo
los lobos.

¡Sobre todo el lobo que hay
detrás de la valla!

And what is that behind the horses?

She is scared of that big dragon watching her.

¿Y qué es eso que está detrás de los caballos?

Ella tiene miedo de ese enorme dragón que la está observando.

Susie continues on her way. She sees eyes
watching her from the hayfield. That's scary!

Susie continúa su camino. Ve unos ojos que la
observan desde el henal. ¡Dan miedo!

Susie finally makes it to the village. She buys butter, flour, and cherries. She is scared when she thinks about going all the way back home.

It's already getting dark!

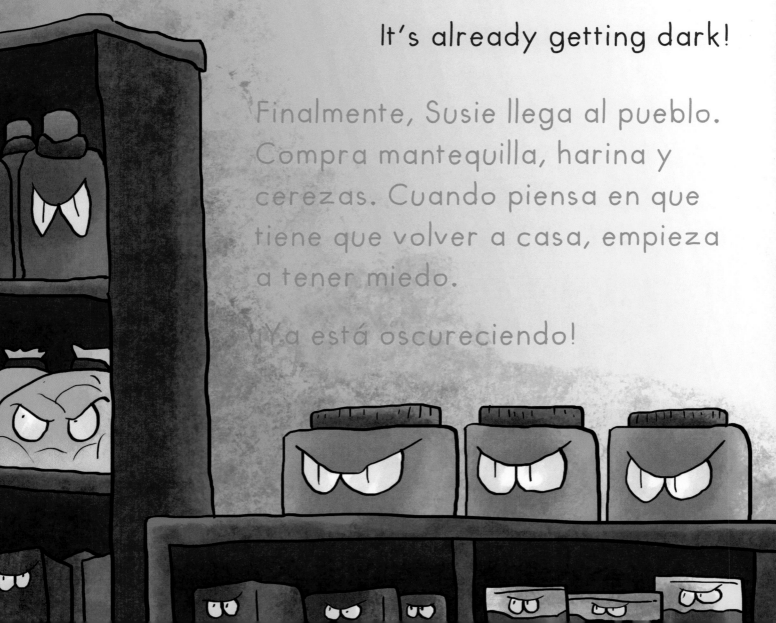

Finalmente, Susie llega al pueblo. Compra mantequilla, harina y cerezas. Cuando piensa en que tiene que volver a casa, empieza a tener miedo.

¡Ya está oscureciendo!

Susie is lucky! Her grandpa comes along the way with his bicycle. He lets her sit on the back. So they can go home together!

¡Susie tiene suerte! Su abuelo se acerca por el camino en bicicleta y la deja sentarse en la parte de atrás. ¡Así que pueden irse a casa juntos!

They pass the hay rolls in the field, but there are no eyes watching them. They also meet the wolf that is just a little dog.

Pasan los rollos de heno del campo, pero ya no hay ojos que los observen. Además, se encuentran con el lobo que, en realidad, es solo un perrito.

They stop by the horses to feed them.
There is no dragon around.

Se detienen junto a los caballos para darles de comer. ¡No hay ningún dragón por el lugar!

They see the friendly woman. They ride through the dark forest with the mysterious shadows and across the field with the scarecrows.

But where are they now?

Ven a la amable señora. Recorren el oscuro bosque lleno de misteriosas sombras y atraviesan el campo donde estaban los espantapájaros.

¿Pero dónde están ahora?

Where are all the monsters I saw?
Susie wonders.

¿Dónde están todos los monstruos que vi? —se pregunta Susie.

She realizes they are all gone.
"It is all imagination," her grandpa
says.

Se da cuenta de que todos se han ido.
—Todo está en tu imaginación —le
dice su abuelo.

COLORiNG PiCS

What is Susie scared of?

Bilingual Books to Remember

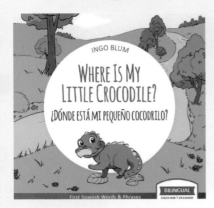

ISBN 978-1983139369

ISBN 978-1983139826

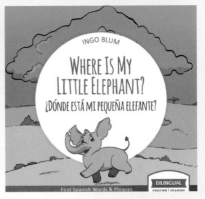

ISBN 978-1983140709

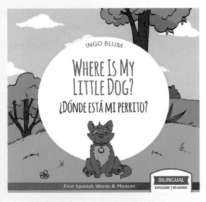

ISBN 978-1983140907

 ingoblumauthor

 ingosplanet

 ingosplanet

Get my 5 eBook Starter
Library in English for FREE on
bit.ly/5freebooks